MAINLINE STEAM
IN THE
SEVENTIES

A Pictorial story of
Preserved Locomotives
at work.

by
Rex Coffin

6000 Locomotive
Association

Foreword by David Shepherd and Peter Prior

Designed and produced by Oxford Publishing Co., Oxford

SBN 0 9503120 1 0

Printed in the City of Oxford by B. H. Blackwell (Printing) Oxford

Photo reproduction and offset plates
by Oxford Litho Plates Ltd. Oxford.

Published by the 6000 Locomotive Association, Hereford

INTRODUCTION

Mainline Steam in the Seventies is a look at some of the steam engines of the preservation era that have once more returned to an active life on the main lines of British Rail.

The story which, happily at this time, appears to have no end, must, of course, start with the emergence of *King George V* in October, 1971. That never-to-be-forgotten week of the 'experimental' runs starting and finishing at Hereford and embracing Birmingham, London and Swindon with 'KGV' hauling Bulmers Cider Train not only carried the hopes of Peter Prior who had done so much in negotiating with B.R. to bring about, albeit at that time, a temporary relaxation of the steam ban but also the hopes and aspirations of everyone else in the preservation movement who was involved with a possible 'runner' on the main line.

The successful outcome of the experiment can now be seen from time to time on selected routes throughout the country as, following the assessment of 6000's week-long tour, British Rail permanently lifted the ban and gave the green light for more locomotives to take to their rails and, apart from one or two minor problems, the resulting 'Return to Steam' programme of special trains has been a great success.

In compiling *Mainline Steam in the Seventies* I would like to pay tribute to the organisers of these excursions onto the main line because I think, generally speaking, the public do not realise how much hard work is involved in the planning and running of these special trains. Firstly, a plan has to be drawn up for a tour and if another locomotive is involved agreement reached for its use. An application detailing the outline proposal for the tour has then to be submitted to the B.R.B. for their approval and charges. Once approval has been given the detailed work of planning the tour including such aspects as provision of water, depot facilities, insurance, etc. for the locomotives has to be undertaken together with the more traditional planning of train formation, catering and itineraries, etc. These plans are then discussed in detail with the organising region of British Rail involved and once agreement is reached a preliminary budget is drawn up and the publicity issued to magazines and newspapers, etc. for the actual selling of the train. Basically a 'Return to Steam' tour means an extremely high work-load for the Society involved, with British Rail playing their part too. They have to provide the footplate crews, coaching stock and traction for the non-steam legs.

It is only after all these arrangements have been finalised and the final costs worked out that the ticket price and the charge to the passenger can be worked out. I have heard and read many complaints about the price of tickets for steam tours but, as I know from personal experience, the price charged only just covers the costs.

All the locomotives that have returned to steam have done so through the efforts of the Society members involved together with, in two or three notable examples, well-known personalities in business and industrial fields, and it is to their willingness to make the locomotives available often after many hours of hard work and without any financial reward that *Mainline Steam in the Seventies* is available and, together with British Rail, reality. I cannot praise their efforts enough and I thank them for the pleasure they have brought me and thousands of others.

Rex Coffin
June 1974

1. The return of *King George V* to the main line in October, 1971 is well known, having been widely reported in the press at the time, and I feel that most readers will know the details of this historic event. However, I think that these pictures had to be included as this was the start of Steam in the Seventies. I positioned myself at the entrance of the Severn Tunnel as I was sure that this position would produce a good picture. The weather was fine and I was very pleased with the result. Here *King George V* emerges from the Bristol side of the tunnel and is then seen pulling away towards Pilning. October 2nd, 1971.

2. At the end of a triumphant week, *King George V* returning home to Hereford, is seen passing North Somerset Junction, Bristol and receiving a wave from a little boy who, no doubt, had never seen a steam engine before. October 9th, 1971.

3. During its lifetime, *King George V* has been seen in many films and it was for this reason that, on November 11th, 1972, she was steamed for a special run between Hereford and Newport to allow a film crew to obtain material for the 'Golden Age of Steam'. Here she sets back onto B.R. metals outside the Railway Centre at Bulmers, Hereford.

4. To enable the film crew to obtain sufficient footage, the train made a number of stops. In this view it was halted at Pontrilas Signal Box, some twelve miles south of Hereford. Pontrilas used to be the junction for the Golden Valley Branch.

5.

Coming and going at Banbury, another triumph for preservation. Great Western Society Loco No. 6998 *Burton Agnes Hall*, heads towards Tyseley from Didcot in 1972, with her first 'Return to Steam' tour.

6. *Burton Agnes Hall* was also involved in the Centenary celebrations of the Maidenhead-Marlow Branch on July 15th, 1973, together with No. 6106 and No. 1450. They worked on a continual service from mid-morning to early evening from Maidenhead to Marlow via Bourne End.

7.

No. 6106, another Great Western Society engine, picks up passengers in Maidenhead Station and, a few minutes later, in pouring rain leaves for Bourne End.

8.   No. 6106 at speed near Cookham and (below) here arriving at Bourne End.

9.

At Bourne End the 'Marlow Donkey', as the train was affectionately known, took passengers on to Marlow in an auto-train hauled by No. 1450 which was on loan from the Dart Valley Railway for the day. Here No. 1450 is seen leaving Marlow for the return journey and, below, triumphantly entering Bourne End.

10. *Burton Agnes Hall* was attached to the Maidenhead end of the train whilst No. 6106 was at the other end. Below, the single line staff is given up at Maidenhead. Note the bicycle clips on the fireman's overalls—a very familiar sight in steam days.

11.   *Burton Agnes Hall* speeds through Cookham during the Centenary celebrations.

12. On June 24th, 1973, the Great Western Society were responsible for the 'Great Western Returns' tour. This involved *Burton Agnes Hall* once more, and on this occasion *King George V*. Here the train joins the Hereford-Shrewsbury line at Shelwick Junction on the down journey from Didcot.

13.

This particular tour was unfortunately not a happy one for *Burton Agnes Hall*. Whilst *King George V* worked the train on to Shrewsbury, through Shelwick Junction, *Burton Agnes Hall* was taken to Bulmers for both servicing and emergency repairs to a blowing steam pipe. These repairs were made by members of the Great Western Society who were assisted by 6000 Association depot staff.

14. The work on the steam pipe was completed in time for the engine to take its place at the head of the train at Hereford which *King George V* is seen here bringing back to Hereford through Moreton-on-Lugg.

15.   With steam pipe repaired and no longer blowing, this picture, taken from the Downside Goods Shed, shows *Burton Agnes Hall* ready to leave Hereford.

16.   Pulling well, the locomotive heads out of Hereford, but only to be dogged with further bad luck, she blew a superheater tube near Worcester and had to be assisted back to Didcot.

17.

October 14th, 1972, was the first occasion that two preserved locomotives were used together on the main line. These two were No. 5596 *Bahamas* and *King George V*. No. 5596, owned by the Bahamas Loco Society and kept at Dinting, worked from Shrewsbury to Hereford whilst *King George V* worked the Hereford-Newport leg of the 'Welsh Borderman' tour. *Bahamas* leans to the curve at Shelwick Junction and later setting back through Hereford Barr's Court for servicing at Bulmers.

18.

The northbound changeover at Hereford. *King George V* moves off whilst *Bahamas* waits in the middle road to work the train back to Shrewsbury and, a little later, moves smoothly away from Barr's Court.

19.   Another locomotive involved with *King George V*, this time during 1973, was No. 92203 *Black Prince*, owned by David Shepherd. It took part in the Wirral Rail Circle 'Royal Giants' tour on May 19th, working the train from Oxford to Hereford. *King George V* worked its 'home ground' to Newport and back.

20.   Having been serviced at Bulmers No. 92203 ran back through Barr's Court station, past Aylestone Hill signal box, then crossing to the up relief line and coming to stand at the north end of the station to await the arrival of *King George V*, with the returning tour train from Newport.

21. Another view of the 'royal' changeover. Alas, the semaphore signals and the signal box have now disappeared under a rationalisation and signalling programme which was just getting under way at the time.

22. In heavy rain, *Black Prince* leaves Hereford for Worcester with the final steam leg of the 'Royal Giants'.

23.   *Black Prince* made a very important main line appearance in November, 1973, when she moved to her permanent home at Cranmore in Somerset. Stock and locomotives were moved from Eastleigh to Westbury on November 10th and then, early in the morning of Sunday, 11th, travelled the last few miles to Cranmore. The above view was taken not long after the train had left the main line, south of Frome, and below, *Black Prince* coupled with 'Schools' class *Stowe* arrives at Cranmore station.

24.   No. 75029 *The Green Knight*, David Shepherd's second locomotive arrives.

25. 'Schools' class No. 928 *Stowe*, jointly owned by David Shepherd and Lord Montagu, although not in steam, completed the journey behind No. 92203 without incident. Perhaps Southern fans will once again see this famous 4-4-0 back on main line duty in the not-too-distant future.

26.   *Green Knight* helps with the shunting. Proud owner, David Shepherd, poses with his engines.

27. Two nostalgic views inside the new shed, recapturing the atmosphere that was so much part of an enthusiast's way of life.

28.   This view shows the care and feeling that went into the design of the new home for these engines. Designed with the G.W.R. very much in mind, it also blends in with the local countryside and, no doubt, will prove to be very much an enthusiast's Mecca in the future.

29.   On July 19th, 1973, two L.N.E.R. engines were involved in Locomotive Club of Great Britain specials,
steam hauled between Tyseley and Didcot. No. 4498 *Sir Nigel Gresley*, owned by the A4 Locomotive
Society with its home in Co. Durham, is seen passing Radley on its way to Tyseley.

30. The other engine, No. 4771 *Green Arrow*, owned by British Rail and one of the engines that will be on view at the York Museum when completed in 1975, is also seen working to Tyseley near Radley.

31. Seen opposite is No. 4472 *Flying Scotsman* leaving Bristol on its way to the Torbay Railway Co., whilst on this page she is seen again passing through Bristol on her return from her successful "work" in Devon. Note the two privately owned and beautifully restored GE1 and CR41 coach saloons.

32. September 22nd, 1973, was a special day for railway enthusiasts. It was a first for the 6000 Locomotive Association with *Flying Scotsman* and *King George V* double heading the 'Atlantic Venturers Express' between Newport and Shrewsbury. *King George V* worked the Cider Train from Hereford to Newport and then posed with *Flying Scotsman* in the Fish Jetty Siding at Newport to await the arrival of their train from Plymouth.

33. Nearing the top of Llanvihangel Bank with 'Scotsman' heading the fifteen-coach train.

34. At Hereford the engines were watered by tenders from the local fire brigade and the headboard was changed over as *King George V* was to lead for the rest of the journey to Shrewsbury.

35.   Driver Arthur Sankey keeps the 'King' at its maximum permitted speed of 60 m.p.h., whilst a clear road is seen from the fireman's side for the train's passage through Leominster.

36. A first-ever photographic run past in the 'Return to Steam' programme on British Rail was made at Craven Arms where the Central Wales line joins the main line from Shrewsbury-Hereford.

37. When the train reached Shrewsbury, *King George V* went to Crewe Bank sidings for water from Shrewsbury Fire Station and *Flying Scotsman* took the Bulmers Cider Train on to Manchester where it continued with an exhibition and promotional tour of the north.

38. With a full tender, *King George V* stands at Abbey Foregate ready to set back on the train for the return to Newport.

39.   A large crowd gathered to watch the departure from Shrewsbury.

40.   The daylight nearly gone, the working party pull coal forward for the last leg from Hereford to Newport and another successful steam day draws to an end.

41. No. 4472 *Flying Scotsman* worked a private charter train from Stratford-on-Avon to Didcot via Banbury
     on October 20th, 1973. A final polish to the windows from the driver and 'Scotsman' is ready to leave
     Stratford.

42.   Passing Great Bourton and taking water at Banbury.

43.   Leaving Banbury for Didcot.

44. On March 22nd, 1974, *King George V* went to Swindon to be weighed and balanced. Here she is seen in Winterbourne Cutting near Bristol.

45. After weighing, *King George V* was put on public display at Swindon as part of the Commemoratives to mark the end of Swindon as a Borough. This view was taken from the Works Manager's office window.

46. As a fitting tribute to mark the end of the Borough, Swindon Corporation had chartered a partly steam-hauled special from Swindon to Tyseley via Didcot but, because of restrictions, the special was Diesel hauled to Didcot. This meant that the 'King' had to work to Didcot on the 24th ready to take the train to Tyseley, and is seen here leaving Swindon on the Sunday evening.

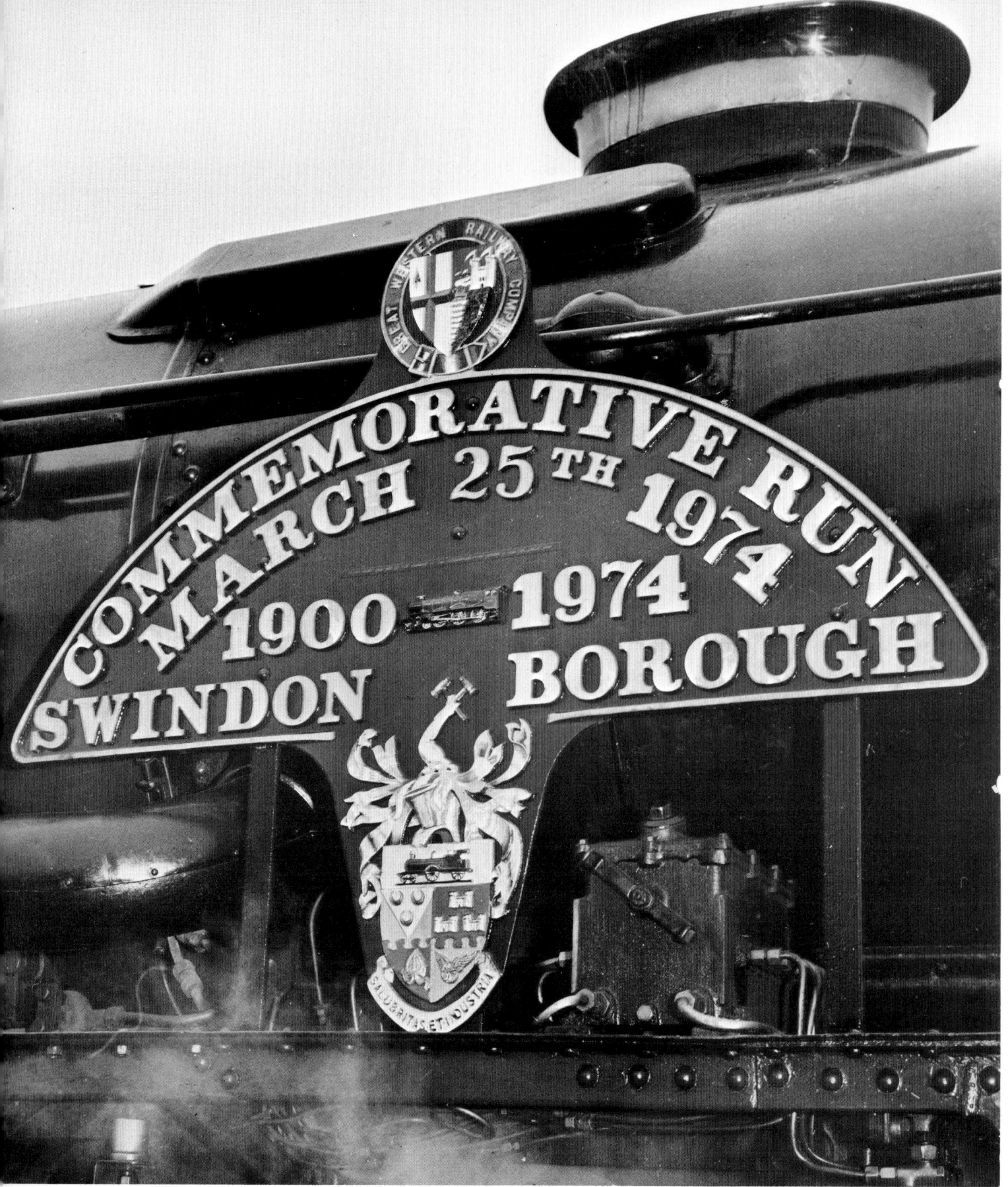

47. The 25th of March, the day of the special run, dawned very misty. Having left the Great Western Society Depot at Didcot, *King George V* joined the special train at Didcot West Curve, watched by a Television cameraman.

48. At Tyseley the passengers left the train and made their way to the Birmingham Railway Museum whilst *King George V* worked forward with the empty stock and then set back into Tyseley depot, where, with the help of volunteers it was turned on the old Roundhouse turntable.

49.   After turning and watering, the 'King' made its way back to the carriage sidings for the return trip. This
picture was taken from the top of one of the floodlights.

50.   Having picked the empty train up, *King George V* made its way back to Tyseley station for the passengers to board.

51. After a perfect run back to Didcot, the train was stopped at Didcot East Junction where *King George V* was uncoupled to go back to the Great Western Society Depot. The train then made its way back, Diesel hauled by *Western Fusilier*, to Swindon.

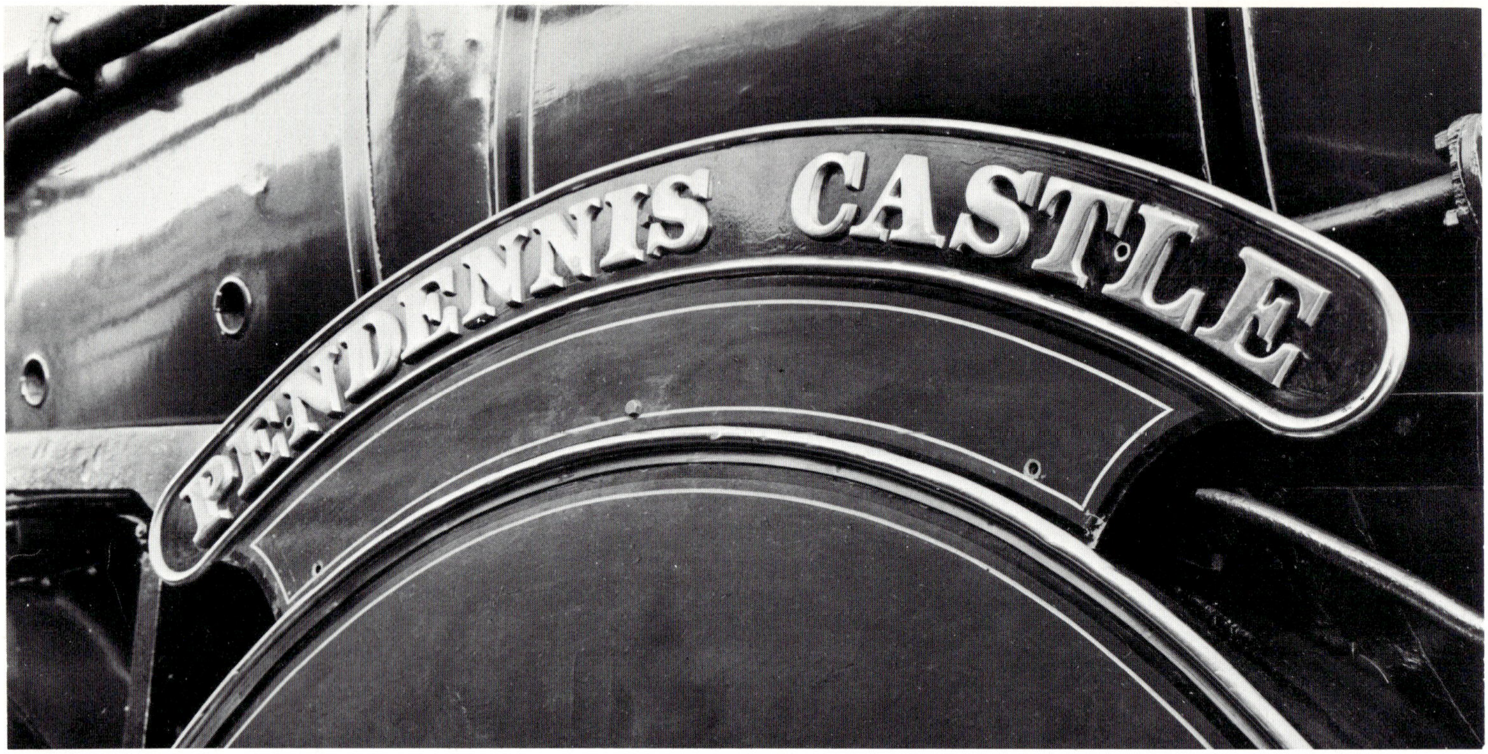
PENDENNIS CASTLE

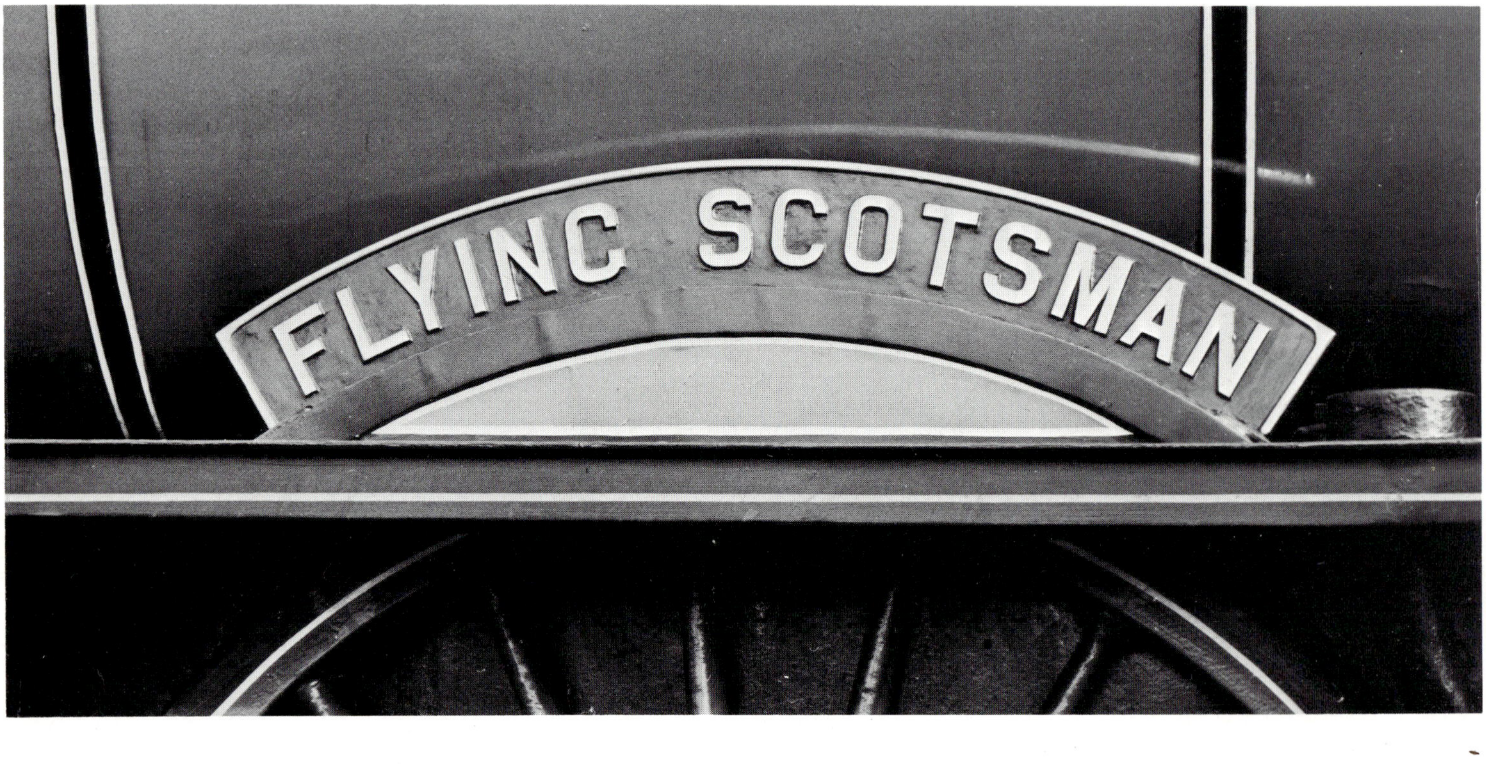
FLYING SCOTSMAN

52. *Pendennis Castle* and *Flying Scotsman*, photographed at their home shed of Market Overton, made a fairly extensive tour during April 1974. This involved their working several trains between Newport and Shrewsbury and also appearing at Bulmers for the 6000 Association Open Day on April 15th where they were a tremendous success.

53. *Flying Scotsman* made its way to Hereford through Bristol Parkway on the night of March 31st, whilst the following day *Pendennis Castle* came down on the Lydney-Severn Tunnel Junction route and passed under the Wye bridge.

54. After spending nearly a week in Hereford, both engines worked to Newport on April 6th and are seen here setting back into Newport after crossing over at East Usk Junction.

55.
At Newport, both engines were watered and then moved into the Fish Jetty Sidings to wait for their trains.

56. *Flying Scotsman* was first away hauling an excursion from Swansea and is here seen passing Llantarnam Junction followed one hour later by *Pendennis Castle*, nearing the top of Llanvihangel Bank with a Northampton excursion.

57. Both engines worked right through to Shrewsbury and then returned on opposite trains with No. 4472 now carrying the headboard. "The Flying Scotsman", works through Pontypool Road on its way back to Newport with the returning Northampton train. *Note.* No. 4472's second tender is now in Standard B.R. coach livery, and this makes it no longer unsightly behind the locomotive.

58. On arrival at Newport, 'Scotsman' was put into the Fish Jetty Sidings for the night, whilst *Pendennis Castle* worked back to Hereford.

59. On Sunday, April 7th, *Flying Scotsman* worked a private charter train which started at Kensington from Newport to Hereford, passing Pandy (above) and then arriving at Hereford.

60. *Pendennis Castle*, after spending the night at Bulmers, waited for the arrival of *Flying Scotsman* in Salop Dock Siding, Hereford. 'Scotsman' then came off the charter special and *Pendennis Castle* took charge.

61. *Pendennis Castle* makes an impressive start out of Hereford on its way to Shrewsbury with the final steam leg of the special. The second coach is a G.W.R. special saloon, No. 9004, and is just outshopped from York B.R.E.L. in Chocolate and Cream livery.

62. After a further week in Hereford, the two engines took part in the 6000 Association Open Day and are here being shunted by the Worcester Locomotive Society Pannier Tank, No. 5786, which although not on the mainline running list, is typical of the small engines that give assistance to their larger sisters in the role of depot pilots and this lends support to Mainline Steam.

63.   These views will give some idea how many visitors the engines attracted and allowed them to see Mainline Steam at close quarters.

64. *Pendennis Castle* carrying the 'Bristolian' headboard heads the Cider Train during the Open Day.

65.   Working home to Market Overton after nearly three weeks' work.

66.   Both views were taken on the Severn Tunnel-Lydney line as the engines passed under the Wye bridge.

67. No. 35028 *Clan Line* was another engine that made a very successful first outing on the mainline. On April 27th, 1974, she worked from Basingstoke to Westbury via Salisbury where she made a half hour stop for water.

68.   Passing the site of the old engine shed at Salisbury on its way to Westbury.

69. On arrival at Westbury it was greeted by enormous crowds. Here the passengers were taken by coach to Cranmore to visit *Black Prince* and *Green Knight*.

70.   Another view at Westbury as *Clan Line* moves off to turn on the triangle.

71. On June 16th 1974 No. 5690 *Leander* owned by Oliver Taylor and Crossley, was one of the engines used on the Red Rose Special, organised by the Bahamas Locomotive Society, between Manchester Guide Bridge and Carnforth. *Leander* worked the train from Manchester to Sheffield, where diesel power took over to Leeds, steam in the shape of No. 4771 *Green Arrow*, replaced the diesel at Leeds for the final leg to Carnforth.

72. In these two views No. 5690 *Leander* is seen in the modern rather unsightly setting at Guide Bridge, and a little later in the more picturesque setting of Chinley Junction. The leading vehicle is the Bahamas Locomotive Society's privately owned BSK-DRC 99300 coach.

73. Hard working Worcester Locomotive Society Pannier Tank No. 5786 shunting at Bulmers prior to a mainline run.

74.   Helping out with the Cider Train during an Open Day.

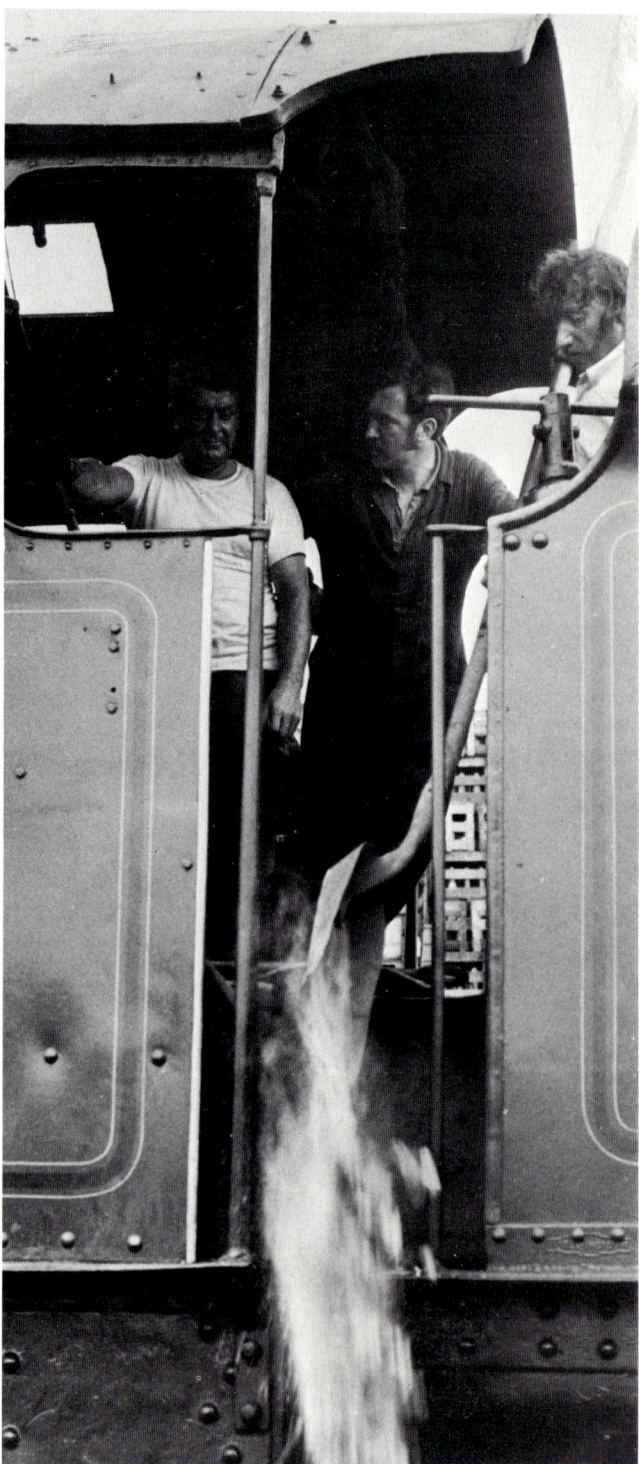

75. When all the crowds have gone, when the excursions, the charters, the specials, call them what you like, have been run, the volunteers will still be there clearing the firebox or dropping the fire. All I can say is—thank you and keep up the good work, lads!